In Praise of *Stormy's Words of Wisdom*

"I was lucky enough to know Stormy in person. Whenever he saw me, he would trot straight up and gaze into my face. And smile. What a smile... I loved him and felt his love back. He was a great friend. Now, here, we have his love and wisdom to hold in our hands. We can open the book every day, or several times a day, and have a happy jolt of Stormy insight. Sometimes the tears well up. Other times, I laugh out loud. That's some dog! Thanks, Stormy. Thanks, Laura."

— **Caroline Thompson**, screenwriter of EDWARD SCISSORHANDS
and HOMEWARD BOUND: THE INCREDIBLE JOURNEY

"I love this book! Stormy's profound wisdom is like big hug for your soul. Thank you for sharing your love and light with the world!"

— **Grace Chon**, commercial animal photographer, author of
Puppy Styled, and photographer of Stormy on this cover

"Stormy is not an ordinary dog, he is truly connected to the creator, to the universe, to the spirit world. Of course, without Laura's highly tuned ability to communicate with animals and humans, both in body and in Spirit, we would not be so lucky as to hear Stormy's inspirational, educational, and spiritual words of wisdom. So, thank you Laura for your very special abilities and thank you Stormy for your wisdom and insight."

— **Kimberly Klein** - author of *Hummingbirds Don't Fly in the
Rain* and *The Universe Speaks a Heavenly Dialogue*

"Laura's amazing psychic gift reveals a world rich with wisdom and boundless love from her dog Stormy."

— Arthur vor   : and

²ress

D1484471

i

The Conscious Bond ™ Series

Stormy's
WORDS OF WISDOM

An enlightened dog's
profound insights on life.

LAURA STINCHFIELD
THE PET PSYCHIC®

For information about this title or to order other books and/or
electronic media, contact the publisher:

The Pet Psychic®
po box 420 Ojai, Ca 93024
www.ThePetPsychic.com
Laura@thepetpsychic.com

Library of Congress Control Number:2019914965

ISBN: 978-1-7333437-0-1(print)   978-1-7333437-1-8(eBook)

Printed in the United States of America

Cover and Interior design: 1106 Design
Picture on front by Grace Chon
Picture on back by Mitzi Mandel

Names: Stinchfield, Laura, author.
Title: Stormy's words of wisdom : an enlightened dog's
profound insights on life / Laura Stinchfield, the Pet Psychic®.
Other Titles: Conscious Bond
Description: Ojai, CA : The Pet Psychic®, [2019] | Series: The
Conscious Bond series | Quotes have been previously published
and/or broadcast. | Summary: "This book is a compilation of my
late Australian Shepherd, Stormy's (aka Storm King) quotes during
the last six years of his life (2009-2015)"—Provided by author.
Identifiers: ISBN 9781733343701 (print) |
ISBN 9781733343718 (ebook)
Subjects: LCSH: Stormy (Australian shepherd) | Human-
animal communication—Anecdotes. | Conduct of life—
Anecdotes. | Dogs—Psychic aspects. | LCGFT: Anecdotes.
Classification: LCC QL776 .S75 2019 (print) | LCC
QL776 (ebook) | DDC 133. 8/9—dc23

I dedicate this book to Stormy himself for teaching me such ancient wisdom with humor and grace. He has taught me to be a more conscious, loving person—not just with animals but with people as well. I have been blessed to share my life with him.

And to Jim Crook for always encouraging me to share my work with the world.

About Me

Laura Stinchfield
The Pet Psychic®

 I have been a professional pet psychic/animal communicator since 1997, although I have been speaking with animals my whole life. My earliest memory is of my parents holding our Yorkshire terrier, Taffy, over my crib and having the feeling of her saying, "You are so *small.*"

It wasn't until my early twenties that I realized that not everyone could hear the animals. Now I help thousands of animals and their people each year deal with and overcome behavioral and emotional issues as well as being the animals' voice during illness, death, and dying. I connect with animals in the afterlife and assist with their reincarnation.

I am blessed to have my work help so many and to be internationally well known and respected.

You can learn more about me:
On my website: www.ThePetPsychic.com
On Facebook: www.facebook.com/PetPsychicRadio
On Instagram: @thepetpsychic
On YouTube: www.youtube.com/PetPsychic

About Stormy

This book is a compilation of my late Australian shepherd, Stormy's (aka Storm King), quotes during the last six years of his life (2009-2015).

These quotes are taken mostly from two places: an online publication, where he helped me write a column called "Dear Stormy." People would write in and ask him for advice. The second is from his segment, "Stormy's Words of Wisdom," on our weekly Pet Psychic Radio show.

Stormy had an exciting life. He traveled across the country with me, hiked many mountains, sat on the beach while I surfed, ran beside me when I learned how to skateboard, jumped off boats into the ocean, knew tons of tricks, took agility classes, tamed aggressive dogs when I was a dog trainer, went into hospitals to cheer up the sick, sat on stage while I gave talks, drew people to my booth at convention centers, allowed children to lie on top of him laughing or crying into his fur, gazed happily at fireworks, and survived cancer.

His siblings included a wolf-hybrid sister, a Chihuahua, a poodle, three cats, three bunnies, a blue-and-gold macaw, a cockatiel, two potbelly pigs, and two frogs.

His doggy dad was my late shepherd's best friend. I picked Stormy out of a litter of ten when he was two days old so that he could keep his tail instead of it being docked. I chose him instead of the "pick of the litter" because he had a white streak on his forehead in the exact same place where my late shepherd Lala had some white hairs. I thought it was a sign. He was the first to bark and the first to wander away from his litter. He was an absolute joy from the start. Even as a young pup, he instantly tamed my dog aggressive wolf-hybrid Maia into loving him. Stormy was always smiling, with his big brown eyes and his mouth open in bliss. People and animals flocked to him.

The only time he ever did anything naughty was when I once left him home alone for longer than normal. He dragged the doormat I loved out the doggy door and peed on it—clearly a message of being "pissed" at me.

He was a large Aussie, eighty-five lbs. in his day. He was all black except for two white front paws and his white chest. The white on his head disappeared. When he walked, he looked so much like a black bear swaying back and forth that children would ask me if he was a dog or a bear. One night, I let him out of the car in the country to pee when I heard a big roar coming from the woods. Stormy sprinted out of the woods to the back of the Jeep and cried, "Mom, quick! Open up the hatch! That bear thinks *I'm* a bear!"

He was a sensitive soul. He sat with my friends who were dying of cancer and told them what he knew of Heaven and the angels. He told strangers messages of their loved ones in Heaven, predicted the future for some, and gave advice I could not have thought of myself.

When he was twelve, he was diagnosed with liver cancer and Cushing's disease. He had lost all his fur. We were told he had less than six months to live. But Stormy did not accept that. We believed that, through good diet, CBD, holding positive feelings, and using the energy of the Universe to heal, he could beat his diagnoses. Stormy did just that. He lived another healthy four years and grew all his fur back, dying at the old age of sixteen. One morning, he ate breakfast and told me it was time. With the help of our longtime vet, Stormy left his body peacefully March 5, 2015, at 11:39 am in the back of our '67 VW Bus.

Before he passed, Stormy said, "This is going to be awesome!" He talked about seeing and communicating with so many of our friends (animals and people in spirit) who were coming to help him transition. After he passed, I felt him warm my heart and say, "No matter how high I fly, know that I still love you."

I used to tease him by telling him to go to Heaven and then to come right back. I was joking. The night of Stormy's death, I had a dream of an arctic explorer telling me he was bringing Stormy back to me. He showed me a river, a blizzard, and a white puppy. When I woke up from the dream, I opened up my phone. It opened immediately to Facebook, where I saw a tiny white puppy with the caption "Things happen so fast, puppy #3. Date of birth March 5, 2015, 11:39 pm."

The puppy happened to be a white shepherd bred by an old friend who lived in Poughkeepsie, New York, on the Hudson River. Stormy was named after Storm King Mountain, a mountain on the Hudson River a short way from Poughkeepsie. This white puppy's mom is named Winne Bear Blustery Day.

Of course, this puppy came to live with me. His name is Hudson, and he is now four and a half years old. His story is for another book, another time.

I want you all to realize that there are miracles in this world and that our animals hold secrets and a consciousness that amazes me every day. If you are open, you too can witness these miracles and experience our animals' wisdom.

Now to quote Stormy,

"Feel only happy thoughts, and know that I love you. I'm Storm King. I am the star of my show."

Contents

It's All Love

Stormy at 6 months old with his older sister Maia.

"I had a dream I was flying in the stars. I asked myself, *Is this Heaven?* Then I heard, 'This is the heart of the Universe.'"

"I usually just think my happiness is from the moment. But I just had the thought that my happiness is from lifetimes of experiencing other beings smiling."

"If you feel yourself being negative, remember love is bigger than all of us. Find a little bit inside of you, and concentrate on that. Eventually you'll feel the ecstasy of it."

"Energy comes from your heart center. From your heart, think and feel what makes your heart grow. Be disciplined. Do something to make your heart expand every day."

"Love is light energy
flowing from your heart
to anyone you look at or
communicate with."

"Each moment, you have to find one thing that is beautiful. When I have a stomachache or I miss my late sister Maia, I look to the wind to be soothing or a squirrel in the distance to excite me. I force myself to believe that the angels really do care and can help us."

"Love is when you are happy to see others. Love is when you feel special when someone is around. Love is when you try hard to learn about a new friend. Love is when you smile at someone and be with them even when you really feel like going back to bed."

Stormy with his friends Stephanie and Susie

"Love is when humans notice an animal suffering and do something to make that animal happy. It helps to tell animals how wonderful, smart, and brave they are. It is important not only to help relieve their physical suffering but also give them words and feelings of encouragement."

"When you enjoy life and love yourself, you may find it is easier to relieve other beings of their suffering."

"If you feel like having
a good time, put all the
other stuff aside, smile,
and have a good time."

"I have learned some people treat pets with more kindness than some humans treat each other. I have learned to love many humans for exactly who they are."

"Love comes from the center of your heart. It is calm and caring. Love is feeling safe and comfortable in someone's presence. Love is a sense of trust. Love is magical because it can heal old wounds."

"We can choose to be in love or we can choose to be in anger. I choose love because it feels better."

Friendship and Family Are Important

Stormy, Bean, and Luca

"When you're feeling lonely, think about all the friends you have. Write them a letter or call them. When you make an effort, they'll make an effort. Friends are important. Old friends are still special in your heart even if you don't see them for a long time. It's never too late to reconnect."

"One can always make new friends."

"Family is important. Tell them you love them, even if there is something you dislike about them. Just saying, 'I love you' can make the 'dislike' part go away."

"Feel good about yourself when you are around people who challenge you. Life should be fun, not drama."

"I'm your friend. It doesn't even matter that I don't really know you. I like you all. I'm so happy to be a part of Pet Psychic Radio. I am so cool."

"You think of me once, and you're in my Contacts list."

"Hey, you should put my picture in your house, like on an altar. Then you can look at me and pray to me every day. Do this, because I have connections."

"Value your friends. Pay attention to their feelings. Tell them you love them when they have had a hard day."

Stormy and sister bunny Bean

"Animals come to you for a reason. You learn about yourself, and they learn about themselves. Some learn how to love, how to be nurtured, how to have patience, how to deal with anger in oneself and in others, how to have compassion for every being, and how to meet everyone where they are at."

"All the animals out there, know this: You came into your people's life to change them for the better. Be patient and they'll grow with you. Enjoy them and enjoy your life."

"Never judge anyone's progress. Praise the little improvements in oneself, in others, and in relationships."

"If you concentrate on
the negative in others,
the negative will prevail."

"I have seen a lot of fireworks. I do think they are spectacular, but I am very sad for the wild birds that night because they are always frightened. I try to tell them what is happening."

"It is important to be
kind to other beings."

Joey, Bean and Stormy

"Reach out to people you think are lonely. Dance with your friends."

"I love to see people get
happy when they dance
with me. I'm a great
dance partner. Music has
more power than even
I know. I can feel it."

"I talk with St. Francis.
He wants us to be more
alive in our lives."

Communicate with Joy and Love

"When you're talking with your animals, focus on your heart and believe."

"If you have a problem talking to your animal, go take a shower, and then come back and try again. Take the time to try, because your animal will eventually understand you."

"Sit with your animals and send love to them. If you do that every day, you'll be able to hear them better. You might hear their voices pop into your head."

"Sometimes you'll think, *I'm so confused and bad at this.* And sometimes you'll think, *Oh, my gosh—I got it!* Just trying to understand your animal will make your relationship with them grow deeper."

Stormy saying, "I like walking in the rain, but I don't like the crinkling sound of my raincoat hood so close to my ears."

"I think the best way to communicate with humans is by looking at them and saying what I feel and need through my heart. Most humans like to feel animals near their heart, so they figure it out."

"Listen to your animal with joy. When you're thinking about them, think about them in joy. Joy is the center of the heart."

"Don't rely on the animal looking at you to tell you they are listening or speaking with you. Animals don't always look at you when they are talking to you."

"When you are with animals, pay attention to their eyes. There you'll be able to see their feelings. Don't stare at them—look softly at them, and see if you can see their emotions."

"If you look at me and my eyes are soft and I have my mouth open, smiling, I feel good. If I have my mouth closed and am looking at you unblinking—or if I'm looking in another direction intensely—you are hurting or scaring me."

"Slow down, and ask your animal what they want to tell you. They will tell you what they need. Pay attention to the way they act."

"Some animals can be confused about humans' intentions. It is important to talk to your animal in a quiet environment. Explain your intentions and why they are so. Then your animal can start to understand what right action is as opposed to an instinctual behavior that isn't appropriate."

"I have learned that people have kinder hearts inside of them than they show to the rest of the world. I have learned that people sometimes talk too fast and don't listen enough. I have learned that people get tired when they don't feel like people understand them."

"When you have a problem with someone else, it's important to communicate. Think about your anger. Take the responsibility to communicate with love."

"The words and pictures you put in your head and feel in your body create your life. Be careful. If you think bad things, your animal and you will feel like you're in muck. If you feel good things, you will be surprised."

Out of the Muck

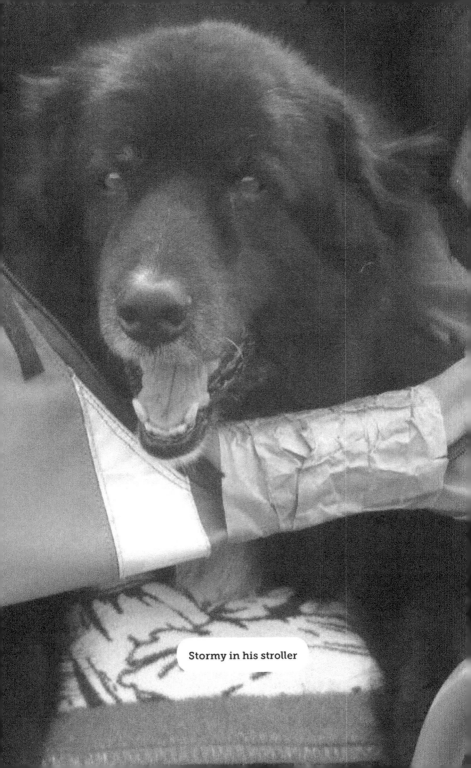

Stormy in his stroller

"I want everyone to slow down and think about their decisions. If you don't slow down and think about it, you might make the wrong ones, and then you'll feel funny when you change your mind."

"If you have a physical disability or a mental problem, keep your chin up and take one step at a time. Enjoy yourself. Ask yourself if you make a good friend. Be grateful. Happiness attracts others. During hard times, it makes it easier to walk with a friend."

"You have to trust your process. Sometimes you'll find yourself in places and situations you'd rather not be. You have to do your best to remain calm, even when you feel like acting like a freak. Stop yourself. If you do some stretches, you'll probably find your way out without throwing a fit."

"I want everyone to know that there's an angel watching over you. If you ask the angel to help you, the angel will help you. I am sure of this. I know these angels."

"If you are depressed, it is best to get up and go for a walk. You may need a hug from an animal. There is an answer to every question. Make sure you're open, so you don't miss it."

Stormy and Serafina on the porch

"When it seems that the odds are against you, people fear their future. Life is what you create. Know this, rest, and then make your future great. I love my life."

"I have something going on with my health that I could choose to fear, but I don't fear it. Because every moment I am alive is a blessing. And I know that, even when you are dead, you are still alive."

Stormy at 16 years old

"Value knowledge and be grateful. When I choose to envision myself well, all of a sudden, I have more positivity coming my way. Greatness is just a thought away."

"Life is what you believe. Fear of the future is something everyone has at some point. If you choose to stay in fear, it will destroy your every moment. If you transform fear, it will make you more powerful wherever your spirit resides. I am happy that I am Stormy."

"Sometimes you have to let go of people in order to learn more about yourself."

"Sometimes we have to walk away from situations that might be too toxic for us. This is okay. Trust your intuition."

"It is best not to do something drastic until you have more clarity around a situation. Make changes from a place of inner love."

"If you can sleep well at night, you have made good decisions throughout the day. If you cannot fall asleep easily, then I suggest you think about the person for whom you are living—yourself. How do you feel about yourself?

What do you want for your future? Sometimes people get worried about what other people want from them, but this is useless worry because those other people do not have to live in their body."

"For most people, success happens slowly. You will have a series of feel-good moments and you will have some discouraging moments, too. If you continue on your path, then all of sudden, you will have a big success.

This is an amazing feeling because you can then look back in awe of all that you have been through and learned. Even dogs feel this way when learning a new skill."

"Everyone feels insecure
sometimes. Believe you
have a path, and you will
always move forward."

"Even the smartest beings make mistakes. Trust your heart. When in doubt, watch. When you watch instead of reacting, you may realize that how you were going to react makes no sense at all. Be patient, and wait until you can calmly make a decision."

"If you make a decision
when you have adrenaline,
stress, anger, or worry, it is
usually a bad decision. Get
a greater perspective. Try
a different behavior. You
might enjoy that behavior
more. If all else fails, take
a nap. When you wake
up, you will feel better."

Stormy says,
"I fell, but life is still good. It's an
opportunity to take a break."

"It is hard not to suffer if your loved ones are suffering. But do stay in joy. There will always be challenges in life. I have learned this by watching people and feeling my body get older. It's our attitude that matters.

Our attitude and our love are what creates our reality. Believe in happiness. Suffering can destroy you if you let it. Happiness can also make you a stronger, loving individual. I choose to love during suffering. You should, too."

Blueprint for Health

"When anyone is sick, imagine a blueprint for health. It's so important. Imagine what it feels like to be healthy and what it looks like to be healthy. And, eventually, all will be healthy."

"I do have one [New Year's resolution] for myself. I want to wake up with better thoughts. I just want to wake up with 'My body feels good' instead of 'Ow!' I have an idea. Each morning, I will feel good saying, 'My body is flexible.'"

"Energy healing is using
the power of the Universe
to heal. I use it for my
sore legs or stomach
discomfort, when I need
more sleep, or when I want
to energize. Everyone
should know how to use
the power of the Universe."

"Whenever I feel a friend being sad, I send them energy."

"In order to be happy, you have to exercise. Also look at Nature and feel, 'Oh, how wonderful.'"

Stormy and Luca always found time to play!

"Stop not believing in your animal's health. Believe that they can get better. Miracles happen every day. Everyone is worthy."

"When you are dealing with veterinary care or animal training, follow your own intuition. If someone's advice doesn't feel right, it probably isn't."

"If you know someone who is sick, keep them in your mind and heart. Picture them strong, healthy, and doing something joyful. Light a candle for them. The angels will see this and give them special care."

"I wish that every animal and human would eat food that is good for their body. I wish for love in everyone's life and walks in beautiful scenery. I wish that no one is lonely and that everyone has a friend."

"I am ten years old; I still need stimulation. If I don't get a job quick, I am going to sleep too much because of boredom. Seriously, you need to teach me something or take me to see people who need dog love. I need a job."

"I want to learn new tricks, and I want to help people more. My mom is really busy. I need to get on her to-do list and on her calendar. Last year, I made two kid friends. I have not seen them in a while. I want to see them again. We love each other."

"Make sure your dog has an outing a day. The ones that can walk should walk, and the ones that are old should go in the car, stroll at the park, or lie in the front yard. No one likes to be bored."

"Know how your body works, send love to the parts that are in pain, and be thankful for the parts of your body that work well. If you want to live happily to old age, this is important."

"When I breathe softly,
I feel like I have greater
insight into my life
and the lives of others.
I feel healthier."

"I have learned that if I push myself, I can walk farther than I thought. Expand beyond your limitations."

"Always remember that just because your animal is sick or has a bad diagnosis, it doesn't mean that you can't live in joy with your pet. It just means you need to be more active in achieving health, and you need to enjoy your time together more."

Maia and Stormy practicing the "leave it"
command with home-baked treats from a fan.

"All animals love treats.
My mom and I wish you
great health and a fun life."

The Dead Are Still Alive

Stormy in his stroller with his siblings
Seamora, Serafina, Makia and Luca

"Spirits communicate
in many ways. You
may hear them in your
mind or feel them in
your body. Sometimes
you may see them in
nature or in the behavior
of another animal.

The deceased know you love them. They don't have any regrets. They are not scared. You don't need to worry about them. It's all heart, laughter, and happiness in Heaven."

"Trust yourself when you feel your dead loved ones around. Dead people and pets are in every home. Yes, you always have someone watching out for you. It doesn't matter if they were an old, drunk parent. They're still watching out for you. In a good way."

"In Heaven, your animal is not suffering. They feel good. They can hear you when you talk to them. We like to light candles for animals on the other side because, in Heaven, candles look pretty. Most animals are not sad in Heaven, and if they *are* sad in Heaven, they find a way to reincarnate."

"If you celebrate your dead friend's life, they will hear you, feel loved by you, and feel connected to you."

"Maia, my late wolf-dog sister, is gone only from her body. Her spirit runs beside me. Sometimes I am jealous that she is young again. I am exhausted from all the fun things I have been doing. The car is the hardest because I am alone sometimes and have no one to talk to."

"Maia is reincarnated. When you come back, you start friendships all over again, but they grow faster. Maia learned how to be happy around people by watching me in her life. She brought back that wisdom into her new life as Luca. I see my friendly eyes in Luca now."

Stormy and Maia's reincarnation Luca

"To help our cat Joey decide if he is ready to transition to Heaven, you should rub his ears. Honor him with love and faith so that his soul will know what is best for him at the right time."

"He may look sick,
but there is still the
possibility for health."

"As a dog, I was born knowing things, confident and full of love, though I used to be a different kind of man in my past life. I lived in Alaska. I was pretending to be someone I wasn't. It's true. I was a human.

I was a fisherman, and I had to kill a whale. It made me so depressed that I decided to come back as a dog. I needed to forgive myself and see the good in people again. I like being a dog better than being a human."

"I remember being in Heaven and choosing my mom. I spoke to angelic beings about living with a wolf-dog and being her teacher. The angels told me I would be a dog that would help many beings smile and feel complete.

I know I chose my life.
I always strive to make
others happy. That is
my job. You have to
make wise decisions
once you are here."

"When I die and depart this life, I am going to come back right away."

Stormy did come back right away. He was born into his new body exactly 12 hours after left his old body. Meet Hudson, pictured here at 11 weeks old.

Fire in Your Heart

"It is important to see yourself as a Light. The brighter you express your Light, the more beings are affected by your Radiance. If you feel dark, shelter yourself. It only takes a few moments to rest and allow the Light to radiate again. Everyone has Light in them. Some people ignore it. Be the Light."

"We're all psychic. Trust your intuition, and connect with the field of energy. You can stand and look at your past or choose opportunity and follow the energy into your future."

"It's important to spend time with yourself. If you don't take care of *you*, your animals will suffer. If you're stressed around them, they might get sick, too. My mom does lots of swimming to remain calm."

"Everyone needs to take care of their own emotions. When a scary emotion comes up, sit with it, and then let it go. You can also take your dog for a walk."

"When you're outside, don't get in your head, don't get on your phone. Get in Nature and say, 'Look how beautiful it is.' Then, when you exercise, your body will say, 'I'm joyful.'"

"Passion is when you have a fire in your heart. Learn how to live with that fire burning. Do not allow your sympathy for others to take you away from your own passion. Make time for both. A fire in your heart will make you feel more alive."

"You have to do something you enjoy in life. I don't care how depressed you are. I don't care how tired you are. I don't care how sick you are. You just have to get up and do something you love.

You could go for a walk. You could go for a swim or pet some horses. You could go out with a friend. If you're feeling depressed, you'd better move your booty."

Stormy in our friend's pool.
As an older dog, Stormy would go
"pool walking" for exercise.

"I really do care about how you feel, but I care more about teaching you how to be happy."

"Everybody should fight
for a passion, share
your love for others,
and help others."

"Trust that spirit guides
you. Know that you are
on the right track. Believe
in your self-worth, and
be excited to follow your
truth. Do not abandon
it. Stay focused."

"Creation is your friend. It is what keeps you going when you feel like you can't keep going. Creation is something you can hold in your heart and speak calmly about. Creation is where we should go when the world feels like it's tumbling down around us. Creation and your vision for the future should be one and the same."

"One of the great things
about being alive is
that you can create any
life that you desire."

"Some people do not
understand that you have
to be faithful and true
to reap rewards. If you
are true and honest to
yourself, there will be love
everywhere you look."

"My purpose is to be your best friend and to help support you when you make big decisions. It is also to help people who are sad to find instant joy in the world. My gift is my eyes. Everyone who sees them smiles, no matter what mood they are in."

"When you feel stressed, you should either write it out, meditate, or go for a run so it empties out of your mind and body. Then, after, you probably will know what you need to do about the situation. So, do it, and then you will feel better."

"My wish for you is that
you know who you are,
so that you can know
what your greatness
is and so that you can
amplify that greatness to
help others. My wish is
that you have peaceful
sleep and good food."

"I know that love is the best emotion to have. If I keep that emotion inside of me, sometimes even my stomachache goes away. I know my mom (person) will always take care of me, and, if something is wrong, she will figure it out. That is safety."

"I know that if people read, their intelligence gets bigger."

"One of my greatest
moments was when I
learned how to jump off
the boat into the ocean.
Prior to that, I could swim
out into the water from a
lake beach. I was thrilled
the day I jumped off
that boat into the wavy,
salty water and swam.

At first, I was scared, but my mom encouraged me. I also learned how to climb back onto the boat. It was challenging. I loved every minute of that day. Everyone should learn new things."

"When I breathe softly,
I feel like I have greater
insight into my life
and the lives of others.
I feel healthier."

"I have some questions.
I have noticed that
many people do not
walk with their dogs.
Why do these people not
want to get their dogs
out to see the world?

Why are people scared to say what they feel?"

"When you follow your divine nature, all the angels work hard to make things wonderful for you. You may find, during this self-exploration process, that you meet wonderful friends and start a whole new happy life.

You may find that you discover different parts of yourself than what you set out to discover. The one thing we can count on is that life changes. Just look at your past, and you will see. Make sure change is for the better."

Gratitude

"When we are grateful,
it elevates our
consciousness and helps
us along our path."

"I have noticed that the people who are grateful for little things are calmer, happier, and more present in life. The people who are always searching for something more to make them happy seem to have more illness and anxiety."

"I am grateful for walks. I am grateful that my mom studies up on which diet is best for me. I am grateful for our friends who take care of me when my mom is busy, and I'm grateful for people who love and take care of Nature."

"People should value
what they do."

"I am grateful the Universe has been created. I am thankful for my mom because she gives me a voice. I am thankful for people who listen to her and enjoy what the animals have to say. The more you listen, the less animals suffer."

Stormy and Laura moments after he told Laura he was ready to go to Heaven.

"In each moment, find
one thing beautiful."

"This is the right moment
to feel wonderful
within yourself."

"I want you all to know
that I love you."

Stormy's adorable paws

LAURA STINCHFIELD

ThePetPsychic.com

Teaching The Conscious Bond™

If you enjoyed this book, please support me by writing a review.

Like all authors, I rely on online reviews to encourage future sales.

Your opinion is invaluable. Would you take a few moments now to share your assessment of my book on Amazon or any other book-review website you prefer?

Your opinion will help the book marketplace become more transparent and useful to all.

It will also help spread the consciousness of animals. The more aware people are of the thoughts and feelings of animals, the better they will be treated.

Thank you!

Take care and be well!

You can also find me at:

www.ThePetPsychic.com
www.facebook.com/PetPsychicRadio
www.youtube.com/petpsychic
Instagram @thepetpsychic

ALSO BY LAURA STINCHFIELD

VOICES OF THE ANIMALS

A collection of insightful articles and stories that will change the way you view and treat animals.